Hiroshima And Nagasaki: Memories And Questions

Congregational Resources
For The Anniversary
Of The Atomic Destruction
Of Two Japanese Cities

Gaillard T. Hunt

CSS Publishing Company, Inc.
Lima, Ohio

Copyright © 1995 by
CSS Publishing Company, Inc.
Lima, Ohio

You may copy the material in this publication if you are the original purchaser, for use as it was intended (worship material for worship use; educational material for classroom use; dramatic material for staging and production). No additional permission is required from the publisher for such copying by the original purchaser only. Inquiries should be addressed to: CSS Publishing Company, Inc., 517 South Main Street, P.O. Box 4503, Lima, Ohio 45802-4503.

Scripture quotations, unless indicated, are from the *New Revised Standard Version of the Bible,* copyright 1989 by the Division of Christian Education of the National Council of the Churches of Christ in the USA. Used by permission.

Scripture quotations from the *King James Version of the Bible* are in the public domain.

Library of Congress Cataloging in Publication

Hunt, Gaillard T., 1939-
   Hiroshima and Nagasaki : memories and questions : congregational resources for the anniversary of the atomic destruction of two Japanese cities / Gaillard T. Hunt.
   p.   cm.
   Includes bibliographical references and index.
   ISBN 0-7880-0348-8
   1. Drama in public worship. 2. Worship programs. 3. Drama in Christian education. 4. Hiroshima-shi (Japan) — History — Bombardment, 1945. 5. Nagasaki-shi (Japan) — History — Bombardment, 1945. 6. Hiroshima-shi (Japan) — History — Religious aspects — Christianity. 7. Nagasaki-shi (Japan) — History — Religious aspects — Christianity. 8. Hiroshima-shi (Japan) — Anniversaries, etc. 9. Nagasaki-shi (Japan) — Anniversaries, etc. I. Title.
BV289.H86   1995
261.8'732—dc20   94-37798
                                                                           CIP

ISBN: 0-7880-0348-8   PRINTED IN U.S.A.

For those who died,
For those who suffer,
For those who will work against it happening again.

Table Of Contents

Introduction	7
Hiroshima: A Dialogue	9
Notes On Sources	21
Order Of Service	29
Topics And Resources For Discussion	41
Week One *What Actually Happened?*	42
Week Two *What Was The Law?*	53
Week Three *What Has Been The Judgment Of History?*	61
Week Four *What Should Be The Judgment Of The Church?*	67
Acknowledgements	75
Index	77

Introduction

In August 1945 atomic weapons were used for the first and only time in human history.

This booklet offers several ways for the local church to commemorate this event. First is a chancel drama, or dramatic dialogue, in which Albert Einstein and Robert Oppenheimer debate the use of the bomb and call on various historical figures to repeat what they said about it at the time. Next is an Order of Service. This, or any part of it, can be used with or without the dramatic dialogue. Then there are four sessions of suggested topics for discussion and further reading for those who want to debate and study as well as commemorate.

George Bell, Bishop of Chichester, denounced the atomic bombings just as he had denounced area bombing earlier, and, much earlier, had denounced Hitler's racial fantasies and idolatrous nationalism. Bell said about the bombing of cities:

> *The Allies stand for something greater than power. The chief name inscribed on our banner is "Law." It is of supreme importance that we, who, with our Allies, are the Liberators of Europe should so use power that it is always under the control of law ....*
>
> February 9, 1944, speech in the House of Lords, quoted in Max Hastings, *Bomber Command;* New York: Dial Press, 1979, page 177.

It was not widely known during the war that many American military planners agreed with Bell on strictly practical grounds.

But liturgy must not be confused with politics and history. Bell could speak thus in the House of Lords, but when he returned to his cathedral he had to remember that the Gospel is forgiveness as well as righteousness, hope as well as contrition. The 500th anniversary of Columbus' landing showed us that the church as a whole has little interest in historical guilt and group recrimination. In this the people are right.

The Order of Service therefore tries to liturgize the atomic bombings as tragedy, not as crime. In the words of one of the recommended hymns, "Redeeming grace has been my theme." In the topics for discussion mitigating factors are presented. At the distance of half a century we still are not sure how to express our full outrage at Hitler's Holocaust, and that must be worth something in defense of anyone on the Allied side. Space makes it difficult to convey the full desperation of that era, but it is central to the story. The dialogue, being limited to about 20 minutes, is an especially difficult exercise in compression, but the effort has been made to include every viewpoint.

Thanks to all who helped or encouraged this project: Kenneth Colton, Mary Miller, the Rev. David Pollock, Richard Minear, the Rev. Susan Hunt and all the others. Thanks to those who gave permission to quote copyrighted material, making it possible in many cases to use the authentic words of real participants.

Permission is hereby granted for any church or noncommercial group to perform any part of the drama or liturgy, and I would appreciate hearing about such experiences.

August 1994   Gaillard T. Hunt
                                 5520 Greentree Road
                                 Bethesda, Maryland 20817
                                 (301) 530-6741

Hiroshima: A Dialogue

CAST:

J. Robert Oppenheimer: Scientific director of the atomic bomb project.

Albert Einstein: Physicist.

Lise Meitner: Physicist. One of the discoverers of atomic fission.

Oswald C. Brewster: Engineer on the atomic bomb project.

Edward Teller: Physicist. "Father of the hydrogen bomb."

Ralph A. Bard: Undersecretary of the Navy during most of World War II.

Rudolf Peierls: Physicist.

Sadako Sasaki: A teenage girl who lived in Hiroshima.

London's Daughter: A child killed in the London Blitz.

Various people of Hiroshima and Nagasaki: Any casting is possible: men, women, children.

Veteran: A mature man.

Commentator: A contributor to *Commentary* magazine.

Host: Jesus of Nazareth, a young carpenter.

PROPS:

Loaf of bread

Communion chalice

Carpenter's toolbox

Shoeshine kit, with shoeshine cloth

Veteran's overseas cap

Hiroshima: A Dialogue

(This 15- to 20-minute dialogue can be done in costume or street clothes, with or without scenery, as a skit presented by itself or as a chancel drama during a church service. If scenery is used, it should be a cartoonist's suggestion of heaven: clouds and sunshine. If costumes, double-breasted suits and other suggestions of the 1940s, except as noted.

The dialogue is a mix of fictional language and excerpts from published material (indicated by quotation marks). See "Notes On Sources" on page 21.)

*(***Oppenheimer** *enters from the front right of the auditorium or church.* **Einstein** *enters from the back.* **Oppenheimer** *hails* **Einstein** *and starts their debate when they are still some way apart and have much of the audience between them. Thus the people they call on, such as* **Brewster, Teller,** *etc., are between them, seated in the audience. The people they call on stand while speaking. They may read the quoted passages from books, magazines, or notes, as appropriate.*

Sadako Sasaki *and the other people of Hiroshima are seated at a plain table, front left. The* **Host** *is seated at the center of the table. They listen quietly throughout the initial discussion.)*

Oppenheimer *(a thin man carrying or wearing an unusually large hat)*: Albert! I need you again. We must do something about those bombs we made. Come with me to the supper and stand behind me.

Einstein *(looks like* **Einstein:** *baggy slacks and sweater and disordered hair)*: I made one great mistake in my life, Robert: that letter to Roosevelt you people had me sign, telling him that the bomb could be built.

Oppenheimer: I don't think the Nazis left us any option. We had to assume that they were working on the bomb. Where is Lise Meitner? What did you tell us, Lise? *(pronounced "Lisa")*

Meitner *(a woman well into middle age)*: At the Kaiser Wilhelm Institute in Berlin we were bombarding various elements with neutrons. I was lucky enough to get out of Germany in 1938. But I soon heard from my colleagues who stayed behind that they were getting strange results with the uranium atom. My nephew Otto Frisch and I figured it out: They had split the uranium nucleus. That released more neutrons and a lot of energy. We discussed it all with Niels Bohr. He agreed the German government could probably turn this into a powerful bomb.

Einstein *(to* **Oppenheimer***)*: But when the Nazis surrendered, you didn't stop. You didn't even reconsider. Brewster did. Here he is. Brewster, what about that letter you wrote to the President?

Brewster: Don't worry, I still carry it with me. It was my ticket into this place. *(reads)* "With the threat of Germany removed we must stop this project. If we use the bomb against Japan we would be the most hated and feared nation on earth. Other powers would watch our every move, and some day eventually the spark would be struck which would send the whole world up in one flaming inferno."

I'm pretty sure Truman saw my letter, and I know Secretary of War Stimson did, because he praised it for its "honesty," whatever that means.

Oppenheimer: I never knew you felt this way, Albert. Do you hold me personally responsible for everything that happened?

Einstein: Weren't you, Robert? What did you do when Fermi wanted to endorse the Franck Report and at least give the Japanese some warning? What did you have Teller do with Szilard's petition that the bomb not be used?

Oppenheimer: I told them I thought scientists should stick to their area of technical competence. Here's Dr. Teller, ask him.

Teller: "Oppenheimer ... conveyed to me in glowing terms the deep concern, thoroughness, and wisdom with which these questions were being handled in Washington. Our fate was in the hands of the best, the most conscientious men of our nation. And they had information which we did not possess. Oppenheimer's words lifted a great weight from my heart. I was happy to accept his word and his authority. I did not circulate Szilard's petition. Today I regret that I did not."

Oppenheimer: It was true. There were limits to our responsibility.

Einstein: Meanwhile, what were those "best, the most conscientious men," doing? Let's ask Ralph Bard. I forget your title, Mr. Bard.

Bard: Undersecretary of the Navy. No one could ever agree how to punctuate it.

Einstein: You also tried to get the Japanese at least some kind of warning before the bomb was used. Did these "best, most conscientious men" consider that?

Bard: I do not think the question of a warning was given as serious consideration by the Interim Committee on Atomic Energy as should have been given.

We in the Navy knew that we had already won the war, and there was no need for the Army to come in and take the credit. Japan was completely blockaded. We controlled the sea and air almost 100 percent.

Oppenheimer: There really wasn't time for thought. That's the way it is with technical things. You go ahead and do it and you argue about what to do about it only after you have had your technical success.

Einstein: I notice nationality didn't make any difference. Here's Rudolf Peierls. Why didn't you go back to Oxford, Dr. Peierls, when the Nazi threat was out of the way?

Peierls: I have been asked many times why I continued working for the project when the bomb was no longer needed as a deterrent, and whether I felt happy about developing a weapon that was going to be used to cause unprecedented destruction and suffering .... The leaders, I felt, were also intelligent men of good will and would try to make wise and humane decisions. In retrospect I have to admit that these views were a little naive.

We know now that the Americans had cracked the Japanese codes, and we know that they had intercepted diplomatic messages saying that the Japanese were ready to surrender if they could keep their emperor.

And in the end, that's what happened: After two atomic bombs, and after Russia entered the war against them, the Japanese still waited for assurances they could keep the emperor, and it was only after they got such assurances that they stopped fighting.

Oppenheimer *(drops some of his urbanity, advances to* **Einstein** *and speaks with conviction)*: Albert, this is all history.

I want to talk about the future. You insist on bringing up the ugly past, when things were done that we all regret. So let's look at the past, in *all* its ugliness. I can cite witnesses, too. Here's what President Truman said:

(He reads) "... General Marshall then estimated that, since the Japanese would unquestionably fight even more fiercely than ever on their own homeland, we would probably lose a quarter of a million men and possibly as many as a half million in taking the two islands. I could not bear this thought, and it led to the decision to use the atomic bomb."

Einstein *(stands his ground)*: Truman! That's the man who said in a radio address August 9: "The world will note that the first atomic bomb was dropped on Hiroshima, a military base." *(pause)* Hiroshima was not a military base, Robert, it was a city.

Then he went on, "That was because we wished in this first attack to avoid, in so far as possible, the killing of civilians ...." — and then he invoked God's guidance in the use of the new weapon.

That half million figure was and is pure fancy. The plan was to land troops on Kyushu, the southernmost Japanese island, around November 1. That was three months away. A lot could happen in three months. There were many official estimates of possible casualties for that landing, *if* it did go forward: Some were as low as 31,000. That's not a half million and it's not a quarter million.

The second landing, around Tokyo, would be nine months away, and no one thought it would ever happen.

Host *(a young man in work clothes, he is relaxed and in command; at no point in the following does he lose his good cheer)*: Come! The table is ready.

*(***Oppenheimer** *turns toward the table where the* **Host** *is sitting with* **Sadako Sasaki** *and other people of Hiroshima. On the table there is bread and wine.* **Einstein** *comes forward.)*

Oppenheimer *(clears his throat and begins formally)*: Before we eat I feel there is a matter we should discuss with you.

Host: Robert, Robert, you are troubled with many things.

Oppenheimer: Yes, I'm troubled. I don't deny my role. I built the first bombs. By our works we are committed, committed to a world united, before this common peril, in law and humanity. But we are not united. What can we do?

Host: Have you met Sadako Sasaki, the girl who made paper cranes?

Oppenheimer: Sadako accepted my apology many years ago. That's what heaven is for.

Sadako Sasaki *(a teenager, not a child; the Japanese can be in traditional dress, such as kimonos)*: I *was* disappointed when I didn't get to finish my 1,000 cranes. I had only done 644 when the bomb sickness caught up with me. But when I got here the Buddha came out to meet me. He explained — it's hard to understand — he said the 644th crane is as valuable as the 1,000th, and the first is as valuable as all of them put together, and it all didn't matter, but it mattered more than anything in the universe. Very confusing.

  He conducted me to the section for children of war. We've got all kinds — Lebanese, Vietnamese, everybodyese. We have four boys and a girl from Oregon, America. They were on a hike in the woods with their Sunday school teacher when they found one of the balloon bombs my people drifted across to America near the end of the war. It blew up and killed them all.

  Here's a girl from the London Blitz. She has a poem about this business of the first and the 1,000th and all that.

London's daughter: It's what Dylan Thomas had to say about what happened to me:

I shall not murder
The mankind of her going with a grave truth
Nor blaspheme down the stations of the breath
With any further
Elegy of innocence and youth.

Deep with the first dead lies London's daughter,
* * *
Secret by the unmourning water
Of the riding Thames.
After the first death, there is no other.

First Japanese child *(need not be a child; could be a soldier, or other adult)*:
Forever she's a girl of thirteen years,
The image of my dead sister in my heart.

Second Japanese child:
Whether or not I listen
Ghosts sob on the atomic field.

Third Japanese child *(with shoeshine kit)*:
Peace festival — none of my business —
I shoeshine. *(snaps the shoeshine cloth)*

Oppenheimer:
I am become Death
The destroyer of worlds.

(Sings "Oppenheimer's Song" to any solemn LM or 88.88 tune, such as Dickinson College, Hamburg, Olive's Brow, etc.)

The stars are said to sing,
"The hand that made us is divine."
What then made this dreadful thing?
Was it made by hands like mine?

A universe of kindly thought
Reflects the Maker's loving plan.
Now all creation is set at nought
By such a mite as clever man.

God's rule we sought to learn,
With observation, joy and praise.
We only learned that things must burn,
And fire now will rule our days.

But how long can we dwell on the past? There must be no more Hiroshimas.

Host: Is the past past? Have the dead buried the dead? *(rises and looks through the audience)* Where is that veteran?

Veteran *(wearing or carrying a veteran's overseas cap)*: When the bomb ended the war I was in the 45th Infantry Division, which had been through the European war to the degree that it had needed to be reconstituted two or three times. We were in a staging area near Reims, ready to be shipped across the United States for final preparation in the Philippines. My division was to take part in the invasion of Honshu in March 1946 .... I was a 21-year-old second lieutenant leading a rifle platoon .... When the bombs dropped and news began to circulate that [the invasion of Japan] would not, after all, take place, that we would not be obliged to run up the beaches near Tokyo assault-firing while being mortared and shelled, for all the fake manliness of our facades we cried with relief and joy. We were going to live. We were going to grow up to adulthood after all.

Host: When did you publish that, Professor?

Veteran: August 1981, the 36th anniversary, in the *New Republic*.

(ALTERNATIVE: You may use a recent letter or comment in the same vein from the local papers. There will be some every August.)

Host: And where is that contributor to *Commentary?*

Commentator: "While we would not think it proper to impose on the youth of Japan pangs of guilt for a war launched by their forebears in 1941, advanced opinion now seems ready to impose on the youth of the U.S. a more searing guilt for the way in which our country ended it . . . . "Modern warfare [narrows] the scope of moral choice into a series of increasingly grim alternatives. The decision to drop the bomb on Hiroshima was just such a choice. It was almost certainly the correct choice."

Einstein: The truth is, Robert, that most of our countrymen still believe what Truman told them, that it was a case of taking a few lives to save more lives. But not everyone thought so at the time.

Robert, I think what our host is trying to tell us is that the past is never past; it will keep on doing us harm until we at least get our facts straight.

Oppenheimer: If I'm to wander unforgiven until journalists and columnists get their facts straight, I will wander, like the Beloved Disciple, a long, long time. *Commentary!* How can a fellow-traveler like me be responsible for *Commentary?*

Host *(laughs)*: Yes, that was unfair. Don't wander at all. Please stay; the table is ready and all are welcome. *(picks up his toolbox, leaves the table, crosses over and moves toward the exit)*

Oppenheimer: Must you go? I'm embarrassed to admit I'm not sure who you are.

Sadako: *I* know you, Master. But why must you go?

Host: You do know me, all of you. Most of you know me as a rabbi from Palestine; some of you have been wise enough to know me in the eyes of a child, or a bag lady raving on the street, or a convict going to the gallows. But you all know me.

Sadako: Why must you go? Stay. We need you.

Host: You do need me. I must go to be crucified again. *(he exits)*

Notes On Sources

J. Robert Oppenheimer

Most of the words attributed in the dialogue to Oppenheimer are fictional. He never expressly condemned the use of the bomb. Up until mid-1945 he could say, like most of his colleagues, "I do not think that the Nazis allow us the option . . ." of deciding whether or not to develop the bomb. (From a February 26, 1943, letter to Isidore I. Rabi in Robert Oppenheimer, *Letters and Recollections,* edited by Alice Kimball Smith and Charles Weiner; Cambridge, Massachusetts: Harvard University Press, 1980, page 250.) And by the time Germany surrendered in May 1945, the technical challenge had become all-consuming. Oppenheimer not only continued working to perfect the weapon, he discouraged discussion among his staff about whether and how the weapon should be used.

Shortly after Hiroshima and the end of the war, Oppenheimer left full-time government employment. His statements over the next few years were defined by the issues of the time. Like most scientists he thought international control of atomic energy was necessary for human survival. He helped create the Atomic Energy Commission, which ended the exclusive military hold over the new technology. And he opposed Edward Teller's "super bomb," the H-bomb.

In 1954 the Atomic Energy Commission refused to renew Oppenheimer's security clearance because of his numerous left-wing associations of the 1930s. Most of the literature on Oppenheimer is preoccupied with this irony, that the United States, in the name of security, fired the creator of its most awesome weapon.

The quotes in the dialogue from Oppenheimer show only his sense of drama and tragedy, not any clear judgment on the bomb's use:

> *You go ahead and do it and you argue about what to do about it only after you have had your technical success.*
>
> > Oppenheimer, referring to the H-bomb, in Peter Goodchild, *J. Robert Oppenheimer: Shatterer of Worlds;* Boston: Houghton Mifflin, 1981, page 210; published in conjunction with the BBC/WGBH television series *Oppenheimer*.
>
> *By our works we are committed, committed to a world united, before this common peril, in law and humanity.*
>
> > *Ibid.,* page 173.
>
> *The scientists have known sin . . . and this is a knowledge we cannot use.*
>
> > *Ibid.,* page 174.
>
> *I am become Death*
> *The destroyer of worlds.*
>
> > From the *Bhagavad-Gita*. Oppenheimer thought of this after watching the first nuclear explosion. Jack Rummel, *Robert Oppenheimer: Dark Prince;* New York: Facts on File, 1992, page 12.

"Oppenheimer's Song" is original here. The phrase "the hand that made us is divine" is from the hymn by Joseph Addison, "The Spacious Firmament on High," No. 409, *Episcopal Hymbook* (1982).

Albert Einstein

The words given Einstein in the dialogue are fictional. Einstein was a pacifist, so he would not object to the role assigned him.

Einstein's insight that $E = mc^2$ explains what happens in an atomic bomb, but Einstein did not work on the bomb itself. His practical contribution consisted of signing a letter to President Roosevelt warning that construction of a bomb was possible. Einstein later expressed regret, but added that the Nazi threat provided extenuating circumstances. (Ronald W. Clark, *Einstein: The Life and Times;* New York, World Publishing, 1971, page 554, cited in Martin J. Sherwin, *A World Destroyed;* New York: Vintage Books, 1987, page 27.)

Lise Meitner

Lise Meitner had been contributing to nuclear physics at the Kaiser Wilhelm Institute in Berlin for many years when she had to flee the Nazis. She stayed for a while with Niels Bohr's family in Denmark, and in 1939, at age 60, she emigrated to Sweden. She was one of the first to explain the splitting of the uranium atom and its consequences. She declined an invitation to join the Manhattan Project and help build the bomb. (*Dictionary of Scientific Biography,* vol. 9; New York: Scribners, 1974.)

Oswald C. Brewster

Brewster was an industrial engineer on the gaseous diffusion part of the Manhattan Project. His letter is quoted in Michael S. Sherry, *The Rise of American Air Power: The Creation of Armageddon;* New Haven: Yale, 1987, pages 326-328. Brewster is described by Alice Kimball Smith in *A Peril and a Hope;* Cambridge, Massachusetts: MIT, 1971, page 39, as "a warm-hearted, explosive individual, totally unlike the popular concept of the imperturbable engineer."

Enrico Fermi

Fermi, like many of the scientists at the University of Chicago, developed doubts about using the bomb. Oppenheimer talked him out of expressing them.

The Franck Report

The Franck Report, a report by a committee of scientists at the University of Chicago, can be found as an appendix in Alice Kimball Smith, *A Peril and a Hope: The Scientists' Movement in America, 1945-47;* Chicago: University of

Chicago Press, 1965; revised and shortened edition, Cambridge, Massachusetts: MIT Press, 1971; and as Appendix S in the Vintage editions of Sherwin, *A World Destroyed*. It advocated giving warning to the Japanese, and urged international control of atomic energy after the war. Parts of the Franck Report appear many places, such as in Alice Kimball Smith, "Behind the Decision to Use the Atomic Bomb," *Bulletin of the Atomic Scientists* 14, October 1958, pages 288, 302.

Edward Teller

Teller's speech is from Edward Teller and Allen Brown, *The Legacy of Hiroshima;* Garden City, New York: Doubleday, 1962, pages 13-14. Used by permission. In that book Teller says he believes it was right to build the bomb, but wrong to use it. Teller is best known as the creator of the hydrogen bomb.

Leo Szilard

Leo Szilard was a physicist who first thought of the atomic bomb in the mid-1930s and tried to take out a patent on the idea. He continued ahead of his time. During the war he lobbied for international control and worked hard to keep the bomb from being used without warning. Years later General Groves was heard to say, "What a pain in the neck Szilard was!" Sherwin, *A World Destroyed,* pages 116-117.

Ralph A. Bard

Bard's June 27, 1945, memorandum of dissent is Appendix O, pages 307-308, in Sherwin, *A World Destroyed*. See "Topics And Resources," point 1.5, page 47.

Bard's first sentence is paraphrased from his interview in *U.S. News & World Report,* August 15, 1960. Used by permission.

Rudolf Peierls

Peierls' first paragraph is quoted from Rudolf Peierls, "Reflections of a British Participant," *Bulletin of the Atomic*

Scientists 41, August 1985, pages 27-29. Peierls was one of the first to do calculations showing an atomic bomb would work. *Historical Abstracts* 42B:4590; Margaret M. Gowing, *Britain and Atomic Energy, 1939-1945*; New York: St. Martin's Press, 1964.

We have also given Peierls the task of summarizing and simplifying the masses of scholarship on Japanese politics and the tedious process of admitting defeat. See "Topics And Resources" point 1.2, page 44.

Harry Truman

The quote Oppenheimer reads is from Harry S. Truman, *Where the Buck Stops*, edited by Margaret Truman; New York: Warner Books, 1989, page 205. Truman's August 9, 1945, address is in *Vital Speeches,* August 15, 1945, page 645.

Probable Casualties If An Invasion Were Needed.

Einstein has been given the task of explaining that the possible invasions were months away, and casualty figures were speculative. The view offered is well documented. See "Topics And Resources" point 1.4, pages 46-47.

Sadako Sasaki

The words given Sadako Sasaki are fictional. Her story is well-known. Her attempt to fold 1,000 paper cranes, her death from leukemia, her monument in Peace Park, Hiroshima — these all serve to personalize the meaningless numbers of the massacre. Perhaps too well. A book like Eleanor Coerr's, *Sadako and the Thousand Paper Cranes;* New York: Putnam, 1977, 1993, should carry a "parental advisory." Many children are not ready for such an intimate view of tragedy. See also Masamoto Nasu, *Children of the Paper Crane;* Armonk, New York: M.E. Sharpe, 1991.

Balloon Bombs

The incident of the balloon bomb is true. In the last year of the war the Japanese released about 9,000 balloon bombs into the jet stream to float eastward toward North America. About 285 were observed to reach Canada or the United States. Not one structure was ever damaged by these bombs. The only persons harmed were those mentioned, five children and their minister's wife, who were killed by a balloon bomb they found in the Oregon woods. See Robert C. Mikesh, *Japan's World War II Balloon Bomb Attacks on North America;* Washington: Smithsonian Institution Press, 1972.

Dylan Thomas

A Refusal To Mourn The Death, By Fire, Of A Child In London

Never until the mankind making
Bird, beast and flower
Fathering and all humbling darkness
Tells with silence the last light breaking
And the still hour
Is come of the sea tumbling in harness

And I must enter again the round
Zion of the water bead
And the synagogue of the ear of corn
Shall I let pray the shadow of a sound
Or sow my salt seed
In the least valley of sackcloth to mourn

The majesty and burning of the child's death.
I shall not murder
The mankind of her going with a grave truth
Nor blaspheme down the stations of the breath
With any further
Elegy of innocence and youth.

> Deep with the first dead lies London's daughter,
> Robed in the long friends
> The grains beyond age, the dark veins of her mother,
> Secret by the unmourning water
> Of the riding Thames.
> After the first death, there is no other.
>
>> Dylan Thomas, "A Refusal To Mourn The Death, By Fire, Of A Child In London," from *The Poems Of Dylan Thomas;* New York: New Directions, 1971, pages 191-192. Copyright, the Trustees of the Copyrights of Dylan Thomas. Reprinted by permission of New Directions Publishing Corp.

People Of Hiroshima and Nagasaki

These poems are quoted with permission from *The Atomic Bomb: Voices From Hiroshima And Nagasaki,* edited by Kyoko and Mark Selden; Armonk, New York: M.E. Sharpe, 1989:

> Forever she's a girl of thirteen years,
> The image of my dead sister in my heart.
>
>> Tanka by Masuoka Toshikazu, page 137.
>
> Whether or not I listen
> Ghosts sob on the atomic field.
>
>> Haiku by Taniguchi Seinosuke, page 148.
>
> Peace festival — none of my business —
> I shoeshine.
>
>> Haiku by Numata Toshiyuki, page 147.

Veteran

The Veteran's speech is from Paul Fussell, "Hiroshima: A Soldier's View," *The New Republic,* August 22 and 29, 1981. (Used by permission.)

Paul Fussell is the author of one of the finest studies ever done on the literature of war, *The Great War and Modern Memory*; New York: Oxford University Press, 1975. He has also considered World War II in *Wartime: Understanding and Behavior in the Second World War;* New York: Oxford University Press, 1989. See "Topics And Resources" point 4.4, page 69.

Commentator

The Commentator's remarks are from Andre Ryerson, "The Cult of Hiroshima," *Commentary* 80 (October 1985): 36-40. (Used by permission.) See "Topics And Resources" point 4.6, pages 70-72.

Order Of Service

Recalling The Destruction of Hiroshima And Nagasaki

Gathering And Invitation

Introit

(The choir calls the congregation to worship with a solemn introit. A musical phrase from a psalm will serve, such as the responses in United Methodist Hymnal (1989) *for Psalm 40 (UMH 774), Psalm 63 (UMH 788), or Psalm 70 (UMH 793). For instance:*

> O Lord, do not withhold your mercy;
> let your steadfast love preserve me.
> — Psalm 40:11 (*UMH* 774)

Call To Worship

(This should precede the opening hymn if the minister is already in front of the congregation. Otherwise, let the minister first process to the front of the church during the opening hymn.)

MINISTER: Let the people of God gather.

PEOPLE: We will come unto God.

MINISTER: Come, from a world wracked with turmoil.

PEOPLE: We will come unto God.

MINISTER: Come, from societies rent with injustice.

PEOPLE: We will come unto God.

MINISTER: Come, from nations set against other nations.

PEOPLE: We will come unto God.

MINISTER: Come, with hearts full of confusion and pain.

PEOPLE: We will come unto God, our Creator, our Redeemer, and our Sustainer.

Opening Hymn *(Any peace and justice hymn, such as:)*

"O God Of Every Nation," William W. Reid, Jr., *UMH* 435; *Episcopal Hymnbook* (1982) 607.

"We Utter Our Cry, That Peace May Prevail," Fred Kaan, *UMH* 439, *Baptist Hymnal* (1991) 269.

"Creator Of The Earth And Skies," Donald Hughes, *UMH* 450, *Episcopal Hymnbook* (David W. Hughes) 148.

"God, Who Stretched The Spangled Heavens," Catherine Cameron, *UMH* 150, *Episcopal Hymnbook* 580, *Baptist Hymnal* 47:
> ("We have ... probed the secrets of the atom,
> Yielding unimagined power,
> Facing us with life's destruction
> Or our most triumphant hour ....")

"Where Cross The Crowded Ways Of Life," Frank Mason North, *UMH* 427, *Episcopal Hymnbook* 609.

"Behold A Broken World," Timothy Dudley-Smith, *UMH* 426.

Collect

O God, from whom all holy desires, all good counsels, and all just works do proceed: Give to your servants that peace which the world cannot give, that our hearts may be set to obey your commandments, and that being defended by you from the fear of all enemies, we may pass our time in rest and quietness; through the merits of Jesus Christ our Savior. Amen.
— *Book of Common Prayer*
1977, page 69

Announcements And Joys And Concerns

Introduction Of The Chancel Drama

MINISTER: No sermon today. In place of a sermon we are going to mark the anniversary of the atomic bombing of Hiroshima and Nagasaki.

We could give thanks that the world has never again seen such weapons actually used on people — and it has been a whole half-century. Or we could say some prayers or sing a requiem for all those who died there, and also for the 50 million or so who died in other ways during that dreadful era. That was a decade so filled with horrible events that there is danger in singling out any one of them, lest we seem to slight the others. Or we could throw open the floor and probably have a lively debate about precisely what the judgment of history should be about that decision 50 years ago to use the bomb.

And we will do that in the Sunday school for those of you who want to pursue the matter. *(Specify when, which, class, etc.)*

But today we will have a visit from some of the people who made the atomic bomb. One of them, Albert Einstein *(introduce the actor)*, did the underlying theoretical work. He was a pacifist, and his only contribution to building a real bomb was a letter he wrote, or at least signed, early in the war. Einstein's letter warned President Roosevelt that the bomb was possible. The other is J. Robert Oppenheimer *(introduce the actor)*. Dr. Oppenheimer was scientific director of the atomic bomb project and saw it through to the bitter end, the actual use of the bomb on the two cities. Both of these men passed on to the next life a few years after the war, so, as King David says, they will not return to us, and we must go to them (2 Samuel 12:23). While we are in the heavenly realm we will hear from some other people as well, such as some of those who were in Hiroshima when the bomb fell. *(Optional: Introduce the whole cast, by real name and role in the dialogue. This should not be necessary to understanding the dialogue, but the cast might appreciate it.)*

So you see many churches tell you how to get to heaven, but only here at this church do we actually take you there.

The events leading to the use of the bomb are the subject of much debate. Most authorities believe from what we know now that the Japanese were already defeated and would have surrendered soon in any event. But in time of war such things are never as clear as they may be afterwards. The existence of the bomb was a well-kept secret, but among the scientists and political leaders who knew about it, many thought it should not be used, at least not without plenty of warning. We will be hearing about some of their objections. So there are many troublesome questions here. There is a lot of material for any of you inspired to follow up on these questions. Maybe some of you will disagree with our guests enough to do so.

Prayer For Illumination

Let us pray: Guide us, O Lord, to contemplate the past with charity; to learn humility from the mistakes of others, rather than arrogance; and to bring to our study of past events enough wisdom and prudence that we may grow in wisdom and prudence. Keep us mindful that your presence in history is something more than the making of history; that sides may win and sides may lose, but you are always on the side of those who suffer. We ask for this in the name of Jesus, in whom are equal the east and the west, the strong and the weak, and even the wise and the foolish, all alike redeemed in a love beyond our understanding.

Amen.

Proclamation Of The Word

(The prescribed Lectionary readings may follow here. Or these readings may be used:)

Old Testament

READER: The reading from the Old Testament is from Judges, chapter 11, beginning with verse 30:

And Jephthah made a vow to the Lord, and said, "If you will give the Ammonites into my hand, then whoever comes out of the doors of my house to meet me, when I return victorious from the Ammonites, shall be the Lord's, to be offered up by me as a burnt offering." So Jephthah crossed over to the Ammonites to fight against them; and the Lord gave them into his hand ....

Then Jephthah came to his home at Mizpah, and there was his daughter coming out to meet him with timbrels and with dancing.

She was his only child; he had no son or daughter except her.

When he saw her, he tore his clothes, and said, "Alas, my daughter! You have brought me very low; you have become the cause of great trouble to me. For I have opened my mouth to the Lord, and I cannot take back my vow."

She said to him, "My father, if you have opened your mouth to the Lord, do to me according to what has gone out of your mouth, now that the Lord has given you vengeance against your enemies, the Ammonites." And she said to her father, "Let this be done for me: Grant me two months, so that I may go and wander on the mountains, and bewail my virginity, my companions and I."

"Go," he said and sent her away for two months. So she departed, she and her companions, and bewailed her virginity on the mountains.

At the end of two months, she returned to her father, who did with her according to the vow he had made.
— Judges 11:30-32, 34-39

The word of the Lord.

PEOPLE: Thanks be to God.

Psalm *(May be read responsively or however is customary. Psalm 120 or Psalm 130 may be used.)*

*In my distress I cried unto the Lord,
and he heard me.*

> *Deliver my soul, O Lord, from lying lips, and from a deceitful tongue.*
> *What shall be given unto thee? or what shall be done unto thee, thou false tongue?*
> *Sharp arrows of the mighty, with coals of juniper.*
> *Woe is me, that I sojourn in Mesech, that I dwell in the tents of Kedar!*
> *My soul hath long dwelt with him that hateth peace.*
> *I am for peace: but when I speak, they are for war.*
> — Psalm 120 (KJV)

New Testament

READER: The New Testament Lesson is from The Revelation to John, chapter 14, beginning at verse 17:

> *Then another angel came out of the temple in heaven, and he too had a sharp sickle. Then another angel came out from the altar, the angel who has authority over fire, and he called with a loud voice to him who had the sharp sickle, "Use your sharp sickle and gather the clusters of the vine of the earth, for its grapes are ripe." So the angel swung his sickle over the earth and gathered the vintage of the earth, and he threw it into the great wine press of the wrath of God. And the wine press was trodden outside the city, and blood flowed from the wine press, as high as a horse's bridle, for a distance of about two hundred miles.*
> — Revelation 14:17-20

The word of the Lord.

PEOPLE: Thanks be to God.

Hymn

> "To Mock Your Reign, O Dearest Lord," Fred Pratt Green, *UMH* 285; *Episcopal Hymnbook* 170.
> Or use one of the hymns listed on page 30.

Gospel

READER: The Gospel reading for today is from Matthew, chapter 22, verses 34 through 40:

> *When the Pharisees heard that he had silenced the Sadducees, they gathered together, and one of them, a lawyer, asked him a question to test him. "Teacher, which commandment in the law is the greatest?" He said to him, " 'You shall love the Lord your God with all your heart, and with all your soul, and with all your mind.' This is the greatest and first commandment. And a second is like it: 'You shall love your neighbor as yourself.' On these two commandments hang all the law and the prophets."*
>
> — Matthew 22:34-40

(Or:)

READER: The Gospel reading for today is from Matthew, chapter 25, verses 34 through 40:

> *". . . Then the king will say to those at his right hand, 'Come, you that are blessed by my Father, inherit the kingdom prepared for you from the foundation of the world; for I was hungry and you gave me food, I was thirsty and you gave me something to drink, I was a stranger and you welcomed me, I was naked and you gave me clothing, I was sick and you took care of me, I was in prison and you visited me.' Then the righteous will answer him, 'Lord, when was it that we saw you hungry and gave you food, or thirsty and gave you something to drink? And when was it that we saw you a stranger and welcomed you, or naked and gave you clothing? And when was it that we saw you sick or in prison and visited you?' And the king will answer them, 'Truly I tell you, just as you did it to one of the least of these who are members of my family, you did it to me.' "*
>
> — Matthew 25:34-40

The Holy Gospel according to Matthew.

PEOPLE: Thanks be to God.

READER: Please be seated.

(It is important that the reader tell the congregation to be seated at the end of the Gospel or they will still be standing when the dialogue starts.)

Hiroshima: A Dialogue *(or a sermon is preached)*

The Response

(After the presentation of the dialogue "Hiroshima," the service resumes with a hymn.)

Hymn

"There Is A Fountain Filled With Blood," William Cowper, *UMH* 622.

Prayer of Confession

MINISTER *(Kneeling at the altar):* We come before you, Lord, as children who have wandered from your household. We have turned our back on your law, we have set up our own idols, we have failed to call on your name when we had great need to do so. We bit eagerly into the knowledge of good and evil, for we were told it would make us as gods. We determined to build towers that would reach heaven. We did that which we should not do, and we left undone nothing that would feed our fantasies of control, of ownership rather than stewardship, and of dominion over all we could grab of your creation.

But the one who loves, chastens. Where once we fell like grass before your scythe and like grapes under your sickle, help us to heed subtler admonitions. Help us to see in our spoiled countrysides and blighted cities your hand laid on us in gentler warning. Help us to see more quickly the motes we can remove from our own eyes than we see the beams, the great public scandals, about which we can do little. Give us, O Lord, a sensibility of sin.

Then may we say with unfeigned contrition that we detest all the sins that separate us from our God, that we have a firm purpose of amendment, and that we beseech the forgiveness promised us, not for any merits of our own but for those of your Son, who lived among us and died a death as horrible as any which human ingenuity could contrive.

Kyrie

>MINISTER: Let the church join in saying:
>
>PEOPLE: Lord, have mercy on us.
>
>MINISTER: Christ, have mercy on us.
>
>PEOPLE: Lord, have mercy on us.

Words Of Assurance

>MINISTER: *(standing and facing the congregation)*
>Know then that your sins are forgiven, and know with Job's certainty, that your redeemer lives, and stands on the earth in the latter days.
>
>Let the church proclaim the mystery of faith:
>
>PEOPLE: Christ has died.
>Christ is risen.
>Christ shall come again.

Passing The Peace

>MINISTER: As a forgiven and reconciled people, let us greet one another. May the peace of the Lord be always with you.
>
>PEOPLE: And also with you.

(Greetings and handshakes all around.)

Offering:
Now let us offer ourselves and our gifts to God.

(Ushers collect the offering while the choir or a soloist offers some music.)

Doxology

"Praise God From Whom All Blessings Flow," Thomas Ken, *UMH* 94 or 95; *Episcopal Hymnbook* 380, v. 3.

Pastoral Prayer

We have dwelt today, O Lord, on tragedy and catastrophe. Help us to draw from that a due sense of our limitations and a proper sense of caution in the unleashing of powers we only dimly understand. At the same time keep us from the dangerous follies of corporate guilt and collective recrimination.

But more importantly, O Lord, keep always before us the glories of your creation and of our merciful preservation in it. Keep us mindful of cities that have been rebuilt, of wars that have been prevented, of souls that have learned to practice the Christian's duty to be glad.

And from that gladness, O Lord, make us instruments of the gladness of others, as our works further your love, and as our prayers ceaselessly call for the coming of your Kingdom, as Jesus taught us to pray:

The Lord's Prayer

Closing Hymn *(This should be more hopeful than the previous hymns.)*

"O Holy City, Seen Of John," Walter Russell Bowie, *UMH* 726, *Episcopal Hymnbook* 582, 583.

"Thou Hidden Source Of Calm Repose," Charles Wesley, *UMH* 153.

"In Christ There Is No East Or West," John Oxenham and Laurence Hull Stookey, *UMH* 548.

"There Is A Balm In Gilead," traditional, *UMH* 375.
"Blow Ye The Trumpet, Blow," Charles Wesley, *UMH* 379.
"Jesus, Savior, Pilot Me," Edward Hopper, *UMH* 509.
"O Day Of Peace That Dimly Shines," Carl P. Daw, Jr., *UMH* 729, *Episcopal Hymnbook* 597.
"This Is My Song," Lloyd Stone and Georgia Harkness, *UMH* 437.

Benediction
Go now in peace.
Go to know the Creator and to love the Redeemer, and to serve the Holy Spirit to build God's kingdom in a suffering world.
Go to do the peace of God and the peace of God will go with you.

(The choir may respond with an Amen, such as one of those in the UMH, 897-904.)

Topics And Resources For Discussion

Week One — *What Actually Happened?*

Week Two — *What Was The Law?*

Week Three — *What Has Been The Judgment Of History?*

Week Four — *What Should Be The Judgment Of The Church?*

Introduction

An enormous amount has been written about every aspect of the decision to use the atomic bomb. This outline of "Topics And Resources" is offered for Sunday schools and discussion groups who would like to study the subject. The outline assumes four weekly sessions of about an hour each, but it can be adjusted to any schedule.

Each week begins with some **openers** or ice-breaking questions. You may want to skip these if your group is already in the talk mode. A section of **narrative and comment** is next. The group leader should read this ahead of time and summarize it for the group. **Scripture** selections are next, followed by **discussion questions**. These are meant only as suggestions.

At the end of each week there are **references for further reading** and **footnotes**.

Week One — What Actually Happened?

Openers

When is the last time you have heard someone say they would have used the atomic bomb had they been in Truman's shoes?

What did you (or your parents or grandparents) do after supper on August 14, 1945?

Narrative And Comment

1. Facts and events.

The bomb has suffered more than most subjects from people thinking about it in the abstract without first learning the details: that the planned invasion of Japan was three months away, that there had already been Japanese peace feelers, that there was no reason to think surprise use of the bomb would be more effective than a threat or a demonstration, etc.

Review this brief chronology:

January 1939. Scientists in Berlin announce that they have split the uranium atom.

September 1, 1939. Hitler starts World War II by invading Poland.

1940. Britain and Germany begin increasingly heavy bombing of each other's cities. The "Blitz" of London begins in September 1940 and continues heavily for several months.

December 7, 1941. The Japanese attack Pearl Harbor and other U.S. bases, thereby forcing the United States to enter the war.

June 6, 1944. The Allies land in Normandy, France, and start advancing across Europe.

Winter and Spring, 1945. The Allies gradually push back the German army, but Hitler insists on continued resistance. He finally commits suicide April 30, 1945, with the Russian army about a mile from his bunker.

May 8, 1945. The remnants of the German military formally surrender.

July 16, 1945. Successful test of an atomic bomb at Alamogordo, New Mexico.

July 26, 1945. In the Potsdam Declaration the Allies call upon the Japanese to surrender or face destruction. The Potsdam Declaration mentions neither the emperor nor the bomb.

August 6, 1945. (All dates are the Washington dates.) Destruction of Hiroshima.

August 8, 1945. Russia declares war on Japan, moves against the Japanese army in Manchuria.

August 9, 1945. Destruction of Nagasaki.

August 10, 1945. A Japanese message arrives in Washington: They will surrender if they may keep their emperor.

August 11, 1945. The Allies reply that the emperor will act under orders of the Supreme Allied Commander. This is the first Allied intimation that unconditional surrender does not mean the destruction of the Japanese emperor.

August 14, 1945. President Truman announces that the Japanese have accepted these terms and have surrendered. Bloodshed does not entirely stop for several days.

1.1. The kamikaze problem: war with an alien and unknown enemy. Why did some American officials believe Japan would never surrender?

The war with Japan was much more barbaric than the war with Germany. There was a cult of military self-sacrifice among the Japanese that Americans found incomprehensible. For instance, the Japanese military revived an idea they found in classical Japanese literature: that an honorable warrior will smash (*gyokusai*) the most precious jewel rather than compromise even a trifle. By the end of the war some of the Japanese militarists were calling for an *ichioku gyokusai,* a jewel smash of the entire nation. This sort of thing, like the kamikaze pilots themselves, kept most Americans from realizing that a large element within the Japanese government was looking for a way to admit defeat and to end the war.[1]

1.2. Should the Japanese peace feelers have been further pursued?

By May 1945, Allen Dulles and the OSS in Switzerland were talking to certain Japanese diplomats who wanted an end to the war. There are numerous studies on the struggle between the peacemakers and bitter-enders within the Japanese government.[2] Here is a summary by the United States Strategic Bombing Survey:

> *Although a core of bitter-end resistance lay in Japan's army and navy until the Imperial rescript was signed, it should be noted that Tojo's collapse and the introduction of peace-making factions into the succeeding Koiso government quickly followed the loss of Saipan in July 1944 .... Koiso was in turn succeeded shortly after our Okinawa landings of 1 April 1945 by the Suzuki cabinet, which was formed with the specific mandate to terminate the war.*
>
> *... Negotiations for Russia to intercede began the forepart of May 1945 in both Tokyo and Moscow. Konoye, the intended emissary to the Soviets, stated to the Survey that while ostensibly he was to negotiate, he received direct and secret instructions from the Emperor to secure peace at any price, notwithstanding its severity ....*
>
> *Based on a detailed investigation of all the facts and supported by the testimony of the surviving Japanese leaders involved, it is the Survey's opinion that certainly prior to 31 December 1945, and in all probability prior to 1 November 1945, Japan would have surrendered even if the atomic bombs had not been dropped, even if Russia had not entered the war, and even if no invasion had been planned or contemplated.*
>
> United States Strategic Bombing Survey, *Japan's Struggle to End the War*, Washington: GPO, 1946, pages 11-13; reprinted, 1976, Garland Press, 717 Fifth Avenue, New York, New York 10022.

The Americans could read the Japanese codes, so some of this was known when the decision was made to use the bomb. On July 30, 1945, for instance, the Japanese ambassador in Moscow reported that he had told the acting Soviet foreign minister:

> *Unconditional surrender is, after all, out of the question for the Japanese Government .... If it is possible to avoid such a formula, however, Japan desires to end the war, with an extremely conciliatory attitude, so long as Japan is guaranteed the nation's honor and existence ....*
>
> The Conference of Berlin, in the State Department series Foreign Relations of the United States, Document No. 1261.

This and similar radiograms were intercepted and were available to the officials in Washington.

We will never know what effect a U.S. statement that the Japanese could keep the emperor would have had in May, June, or July of 1945. We do know that at that time many people in the State Department and elsewhere were urging such a declaration. James Forrestal noted:

> *... [John] McCloy recalled the meeting [June 18, 1945] with President Truman at the White House at which the decision was taken to proceed with the invasion of Kyushu [the southernmost Japanese island] .... As the meeting broke up, McCloy said he had not been asked but wanted to state his views .... He said that he thought before the final decision to invade Japan was taken or it was decided to use the atomic bomb political measures should be taken; the Japanese should be told of what had happened to Germany, particularly in view of the fact that some of their people who had been in Germany were back in Japan and would be able to report on the destruction and devastation which they had witnessed; that the Japs* should be told, furthermore, that we had*

---

*This epithet was widely used during World War II.

> *another and terrifyingly destructive weapon which we would have to use if they did not surrender; that they would be permitted to retain the Emperor and a form of government of their own choosing.* He said the military leaders were somewhat annoyed at his interference but that the President welcomed it and at the conclusion of McCloy's observations ordered such a political offensive to be set in motion.
>
> > James Forrestal, *The Forrestal Diaries*; New York: Viking, 1951, pages 70-71.

But no such "political offensive" occurred.

1.3. Why were many Americans adamantly opposed to telling the Japanese they could keep the emperor?

The columnist I.F. Stone was among those who opposed any concessions. He warned:

> *[Some] would like to defeat the Japanese military, but to leave the emperor and the zaibatsu [wealthy families] in power. But the emperor and the zaibatsu are the twin peaks of Japanese society as now constituted. They represent the development of a highly monopolistic capitalism on top of a feudal society.*
>
> > From a June 15, 1945, column reprinted in I.F. Stone, *The Truman Era*; New York: Monthly Review Press, 1953. Stone wrote for *PM*, the *New York Star* and the *Daily Compass*.

1.4. The invasion of Japan: When was it scheduled and what were the likely casualties?

November 1, 1945, was the earliest possible date for a landing on Kyushu, the southernmost Japanese island. So the relevant figure for assessing the pressure on Truman is the actual rate of American deaths around the end of July: about 2,000 per week.

Official estimates for the human cost of an invasion, should one take place, varied widely. Okinawa had cost about 12,000 American lives. No one has ever been able to find an official estimate on the order of the quarter million or half million or several million American dead that people later spoke of.[3] Those higher figures, as their range indicates, refer to a hypothetical long-term stalemate — a remote possibility which became much more remote after the Alamogordo test.

1.5 What alternatives were suggested to surprise use of the atomic bomb without warning?

Undersecretary of the Navy Ralph A. Bard dissented in writing from the plan to drop the bomb without warning. He summed up his views in a "Memorandum on the Use of the S-1 Bomb" dated June 27, 1945. Bard said, "The position of the United States as a great humanitarian nation and the fair play attitude of our people generally" led him to feel the bomb should not be used without warning. He suggested telling the Japanese that they could keep the emperor and warning them of the impending Russian entry into the war as well as the existence of the bomb.

> *I don't see that we have anything in particular to lose in following such a program. The stakes are so tremendous that it is my opinion very real consideration should be given to some plan of this kind. I do not believe under present circumstances existing that there is anyone in this country whose evaluation of the chances of the success of such a program is worth a great deal. The only way to find out is to try it out.*
>
> Sherwin, *A World Destroyed,* Appendix O, pages 307-308.

The scientists at the University of Chicago formed a "Committee on Social and Political Implications," under Dr. James O. Franck. The Franck Report discussed the difficulties of long-term control of the new weapon and said:

> We believe that these considerations make the use of nuclear bombs for an early unannounced attack against Japan inadvisable. If the United States were to be the first to release this new means of indiscriminate destruction upon mankind, she would sacrifice public support throughout the world, precipitate the race for armaments, and prejudice the possibility of reaching an international agreement on the future control of such weapons.
>
> Sherwin, A World Destroyed, Appendix S, page 332.[4]

1.6. Was there other opposition, or potential opposition?

General Eisenhower later wrote in his memoirs that he had told Secretary Stimson in July 1945 that he "disliked seeing the United States take the lead in introducing into war something as horrible and destructive as this new weapon was described to be."[5] But there is no written trace of any objection by Eisenhower at the time.[6]

Admiral Leahy, Truman's chief of staff, also wrote against the bomb in his memoirs:

> ... I had specialized in gunnery and at one time headed the Navy Department's Bureau of Ordnance. "Bomb" is the wrong word to use for this new weapon. It is not a bomb. It is not an explosive. It is a poisonous thing that kills people by its deadly radioactive reaction, more than by the explosive force it develops.
>
> The lethal possibilities of atomic warfare in the future are frightening. My own feeling was that in being the first to use it, we had adopted an ethical standard common to the barbarians of the Dark Ages. I was not taught to make war in that fashion, and wars cannot be won by destroying women and children. We were the first to have this weapon in our possession, and the first to use it. There is a practical certainty that potential enemies will have it in the future and that atomic bombs will sometime be used against us.

William D. Leahy, *I Was There: The Personal Story of the Chief of Staff to Presidents Roosevelt and Truman;* New York and London: McGraw-Hill, 1950, page 441.

Scripture *(Biblical selections are from the New Revised Standard Version unless otherwise indicated.)*

After Nineveh repented and was spared, Jonah retired to a hillside to sulk. God sent a bush to shade him, but then withered the bush. Jonah was angry.

> *But God said to Jonah, "Is it right for you to be angry about the bush?" And he said, "Yes, angry enough to die." Then the Lord said, "You are concerned about the bush, for which you did not labor and which you did not grow; it came into being in a night and perished in a night. And should I not be concerned about Nineveh, that great city, in which there are more than a hundred and twenty thousand persons who do not know their right hand from their left, and also many animals?"*
> — Jonah 4:9-11

If your discussion of the facts either lags or becomes too heated, you may want to consider the shortest verse in the Bible:

> *Jesus wept.*
> — John 11:35 (KJV)

Discussion Questions

Should the Allies have made, or offered to make, the concession that the emperor could stay? If this concession was right, when was the right time to make it?

Was there any reason at all for the assumption that surprise use of the atomic bomb would be more effective than use after a solemn warning?

Why use a second bomb within three days of the first?

References For Further Reading
The best single source is:

Sherwin, Martin J. *A World Destroyed: The Atomic Bomb and the Grand Alliance.* 1st ed., New York: Alfred A. Knopf, 1975. Later editions are called *A World Destroyed: Hiroshima and the Origins of the Arms Race.* This source is available in paperback for about $13 from Random House/Vintage, 201 East 50th Street, New York, New York. It reprints several important documents, such as the Franck Report and Bard's memo.

Other general sources include:

Appel, Allen. *Till The End Of Time.* New York: Doubleday, 1990. An adult time-travel novel covering Pearl Harbor, Hiroshima, and the war in between, with candid descriptions of much blood and gore.

Dower, John W. *War Without Mercy: Race and Power in the Pacific War.* 1987. 416 pages. Paperback $15. Random House/Pantheon, 400 Hahn Road, Westminster, Maryland 21157, 1-800-733-3000. This book shows how rhetoric and propaganda, both in Japan and among the Allies, dehumanized the enemy and obscured the ability of either side to predict what the other might do.

Feis, Herbert. *The Atomic Bomb and the End of World War II.* Revised edition. 1966. Paperback $11.95. Princeton University Press, 3175 Princeton Pike, Lawrenceville, New Jersey 08648. (First issued as *Japan Subdued: The Atomic Bomb and the End of the War in the Pacific.* Princeton: Princeton University Press, 1961.)

Harper, Stephen. *Miracle of Deliverance: The Case for the Bombings of Hiroshima and Nagasaki.* New York: Stein and Day, 1986. 224 pages. $18.95. Scarborough House, Madison Books, UPA, 4720 Boston Way, Lanham, Maryland 20706. The pro-bomb point of view.

Kurzman, Dan. *Day of the Bomb: Countdown to Hiroshima.* New York: McGraw-Hill, 1985.

Lawren, William. *The General and the Bomb: A Biography of General Leslie R. Groves.* New York: Dodd, Mead, 1988.

O'Neal, Michael. *President Truman and the Atomic Bomb: Opposing Viewpoints.* San Diego, California: Greenhaven Press, 1990. 112 pages. For younger readers.

Rhodes, Richard. *The Making of the Atomic Bomb.* 1986. 928 pages. Paperback $12.95. Simon and Schuster (Touchstone), 1230 Avenue of the Americas, New York, New York 10020.

Rose, Lisle A. *Dubious Victory: The United States and the End of World War II.* Kent, Ohio: Kent State University Press, 1973.

United States Strategic Bombing Survey. *Summary Report (Pacific War).* Washington: GPO, 1946; reprinted, 1976, Garland Press, 717 Fifth Avenue, New York, New York 10022.

"Was A-Bomb on Japan a Mistake?" *U.S. News & World Report,* August 15, 1960. Interviews with Leo Szilard, James F. Byrnes, Lewis L. Strauss, Ralph A. Bard, and Edward Teller.

Wyden, Peter. *Day One: Before Hiroshima and After.* 1984. Paperback $3.95. Warner Books (Little, Brown), 200 West Street, Waltham, Massachusetts 02254. 1-800-343-9204.

> (Order information is from *Books in Print* and is subject to change. You can order with an open check for "not more than" a few dollars more than the listed price.)

Footnotes

1. John W. Dower, *War Without Mercy: Race and Power in the Pacific War;* New York: Random House/Pantheon, 1987.

2. See, for example, Herbert Feis, *The Atomic Bomb and the End of World War II*; Princeton: Princeton University Press, 1966. Robert J.C. Butow, *Japan's Decision to Surrender*; Stanford, California: Stanford University Press, 1954. Leon V. Sigal, *Fighting to a Finish: The Politics of War Termination in the United States and Japan, 1945;* 352 pages, paper $12.95, Cornell University Press, Ithaca, New York, 1988.

3. Barton J. Bernstein, "A Postwar Myth: 500,000 U.S. Lives Saved," *Bulletin of the Atomic Scientists* 42 (June-July 1986), pages 38-40; Herbert Feis, *The Atomic Bomb and the End of World War II,* above; Rufus E. Miles, Jr., "Hiroshima: The Strange Myth of Half a Million American Lives Saved," *International Security* 10, Fall 1985, page 121; Peter Wyden, *Day One: Before Hiroshima and After,* New York: Simon and Schuster, 1984, page 171.

4. Franck took the Franck Report to Washington on June 11, 1945. It is also in Alice Kimball Smith, *A Peril and a Hope,* Chicago: University of Chicago Press, 1965; revised and shortened edition, Cambridge, Massachusetts: MIT, 1970.

5. *Crusade in Europe,* Garden City, New York: Doubleday, 1948, page 443.

6. Barton J. Bernstein, "Ike and Hiroshima: Did He Oppose It?" *Journal of Strategic Studies* 10 (September 1987), page 377.

Week Two — What Was The Law?

It may seem that the decision-makers applied only the ethical standards of total "berserker warfare": Hit the enemy with everything you have, as hard as you can, and resolve every question against moderation. Were there other standards they could have applied?

Openers

When is it legal in your state to kill another human being?

There are probably some laws that are frequently broken or stretched in whatever business or profession you happen to work in. Are these good laws or bad laws? What should be done about this?

Narrative And Comment

2. Law, morals, and military ethics.

There have always been those who reject war altogether — religious or secular pacifists of many kinds.[1] After Pearl Harbor, however, pacifism was not much of a force in American politics. Most Americans were certain that the war against Axis aggression was as just and necessary as any war had ever been. If there were to be any limits, or any alternatives to the berserker ethic, they would have to come from within the traditional law of warfare.

2.1. The classical view: The just war tradition and the protection of noncombatants.

The moral framework for discussing war has usually been the "just war tradition" or the criteria for a "just war."

The just war criteria have been stated by various Christian and natural law thinkers in many ways over the centuries. Here is one modern formulation:

A just war must support a just cause;

It must be declared by legitimate authority;

It must be fought for moral, not selfish reasons, or with right intentions, including the intention to seek peace;

It must be a last resort;

There must be a reasonable expectation of producing benefits proportionate to the harm done;

And harm to noncombatants must be avoided.

This is how President Bush stated the just war criteria in an address to the National Religious Broadcasters, during the Gulf War.[2]

The protection of noncombatants is firmly entrenched as one of the requirements for a just war. It rests on more than the idea that soldiers have consented to the risks of war and civilians have not. It serves the most basic rule of military ethics: economy. The goal of the military profession is to achieve victory with the minimum destruction of life and property. All else is undisciplined and amateur.[3]

2.2. Did aerial bombing become an exception to the protection of noncombatants? If so, how, when, and why?

From its first conception, aerial bombing was offered as a way to shorten war or to prevent it altogether. Either precision strikes would paralyze the enemy's war machine, or bombing would be so horrible no one would risk starting a war.

When war first broke out in the 1930s, with the Japanese invasion of China and the civil war in Spain, the United States vigorously condemned all bombing of cities.[4] There was never any formal change in this policy. By the end of the war in Europe, the discrepancy between professed policy and what was actually happening had come to trouble many people. Questions were asked, especially in Britain. They were not answered. "From beginning to end of the war, ministers prevaricated — indeed, lied flatly again and again — about the nature of the bomber offensive."[5] The destruction of Dresden in February 1945 particularly shocked much of the Allied public.[6]

Sir Arthur Harris, Chief of the RAF's Bomber Command, openly endorsed area bombing of cities at night.[7] The American Army Air Forces insisted that this was a waste of munitions and claimed that their daylight precision bombing was far more efficient. In the last year of the war, however, American resources were ample for bombing of all kinds, and the dedication to precision fell apart in practice. The fact is that the cities of Germany were destroyed, some of them with firestorms as deadly as the atomic bombings. But all of this took place without any definitive decisions, in an atmosphere of acrimonious but largely secret debate, with no consensus as to when or why such bombing would be legal or illegal.

2.3. Was there ever any debate about the bombing of Japan?

The first bombing of Japan was Colonel James Doolittle's raid in April 1942. This was planned as a nighttime raid by 16 bombers (although in the event it took place in daylight) and was offered as a reprisal for Pearl Harbor. A movie about that raid, *Thirty Seconds Over Tokyo*, released in December 1944, gives a good insight into public thinking during the war. The airmen are twice offered the chance to back out if they feel they may think of themselves as "murderers" later. None do. And the bombing we see is all precise hits on industrial targets.

The American criticism of British area bombing was forgotten when the Army Air Forces turned their attention to Japan. Supposedly Japanese industry relied heavily on small contractors in residential areas. And there was Pearl Harbor. Dower sums it up:

> When Tokyo was incinerated, there was scarcely a murmur of protest on the home front. Privately, some insiders did acknowledge the moral ambiguity of the U.S. strategy against Japan, at least in passing. In a confidential memorandum of mid-June 1945, for example, one

> of General Douglas MacArthur's key aides, Brigadier General Bonner Fellers, frankly described the U.S. air raids against Japan as "one of the most ruthless and barbaric killings of non-combatants in all history." [Footnote omitted.] *Such thoughts were seldom voiced publicly, however* ....

Dower, War Without Mercy, page 41.

Japan did not come within reach of sustained bombing until late 1944. The official history[8] says that the commander in charge, Haywood Hansell, Jr., was replaced in January 1945 because he objected to area bombing and wholesale incendiary raids. But a biographer of Curtis LeMay, the man who replaced him, takes pains to show that this was not the case.[9]

The confusion itself is illuminating. The process of debate and analysis did not function as it does in normal times. Public discussion featured equivocation and evasion, and the most important discussions were secret and off the record.

Scripture

> *Thou shalt not kill.*
>
> — Deuteronomy 5:17 (KJV)

> *You shall not murder.*
>
> — Deuteronomy 5:17

> *The wolf shall live with the lamb, the leopard shall lie down with the kid, the calf and the lion and the fatling together, and a little child shall lead them. The cow and the bear shall graze, their young shall lie down together, and the lion shall eat straw like the ox. The nursing child shall play over the hole of the asp, and the weaned child shall put its hand on the adder's den. They will not hurt or destroy on all my holy mountain; for the earth will be full of the knowledge of the Lord as the waters cover the sea. On that day the root of Jesse shall stand as a*

signal to the peoples; the nations shall inquire of him, and his dwelling shall be glorious.
— Isaiah 11:6-10

When those who were around him saw what was coming, they asked, "Lord, should we strike with the sword?" Then one of them struck the slave of the high priest and cut off his right ear. But Jesus said, "No more of this!" And he touched his ear and healed him.
— Luke 22:49-51

> (This is one of the few incidents in Jesus' life which appears in all four Gospels, although only Luke reports the healing of the ear — Matthew 26:51-52; Mark 14:47; John 18:10-11.)

Discussion Questions

Is there any possibility that some of the American planners were right, that the "dehousing" of the German public made them more available for war and more dependent on and loyal to the German government? Is it possible that the bombing of German cities actually prolonged the war?

As long as there is a new, improved missile or bomb that has not yet demonstrated its inaccuracy, and as long as its sponsors will promise quick, cheap, and decisive results, will there ever be any hope that a democratically elected political leader could say no to a proposed bombing?

References for Further Reading

John Howard Yoder is a leading contemporary witness for pacifism. See his works:

The Christian Witness to the State. Newton, Kansas: Faith and Life Press, 1964.

A Declaration on Peace. Scottdale, Pennsylvania: Herald Press, 1991.

He Came Preaching Peace. 616 Walnut Avenue, Scottdale, Pennsylvania 15683: Herald Press, 1985.

Nevertheless: A Meditation On The Varieties And Shortcomings of Religious Pacifism. Scottdale, Pennsylvania: Herald Press, 1971.

What Would You Do? Scottdale, Pennsylvania: Herald Press, 1983.

When War Is Unjust: Being Honest in Just War Thinking. Minneapolis: Augsburg, 1984.

For more on pacifism, see also:

Adeney, Bernard T. *Just War, Political Realism, and Faith.* Metuchen, New Jersey: Scarecrow Press, 1988.

Brock, Peter. *Twentieth Century Pacifism.* New York: Van Nostrand Reinhold, 1970.

Cady, Duane L. *From Warism to Pacifism.* Philadelphia: Temple University Press, 1989.

Eller, Cynthia. *Conscientious Objectors and the Second World War: Moral and Religious Arguments in Support of Pacifism.* New York: Praeger, 1991.

Friesen, Duane K. *Christian Peacemaking and International Conflict: A Realist Pacifist Perspective.* 616 Walnut Avenue, Scottdale, Pennsylvania 15683: Herald Press, 1986.

Teichman, Jenny. *Pacifism and the Just War.* New York: Blackwell, 1986.

For more on the just war traditions:

Johnson, James Turner. *The Quest for Peace: Three Moral Traditions in Western Cultural History.* Princeton: Princeton University Press, 1987.

LaCroix, W.L. *War and International Ethics: Tradition and Today.* Lanham, Maryland: University Press of America, 1988.

Ramsey, Paul. *The Just War: Force and Political Responsibility.* Lanham, Maryland: University Press of America, 1983.

Walzer, Michael. *Just and Unjust Wars: A Moral Argument with Historical Illustrations.* New York: Basic Books, 1977.

On the development of strategic bombing, including the moral and legal questions, see:

Lee, Kennett. *A History of Strategic Bombing.* New York: Scribners, 1982. A brief study of the history of strategic bombing in general.

Schaffer, Ronald. *Wings of Judgment: American Bombing in World War II.* 1985. 288 pages. Paperback $10.95. Oxford University Press, 2001 Evans Road, Cary, North Carolina 27513. 1-800-451-7556.

Sherry, Michael S. *The Rise of American Air Power: The Creation of Armageddon.* 1987. 428 pages. $40.00. Yale University Press, Box 92A Yale Station, New Haven, Connecticut 06520. 203-432-0940.

Spaight, J. M. *Bombing Vindicated.* London: Geoffrey Bles, 1944. Spaight, a British civil servant and air advocate, hailed the bomber as the savior of civilization.

Footnotes

1. For pacifism, see the works of John Howard Yoder and other books in the reading list above.

2. Printed in James Turner Johnson and George Weigel, *Just War and the Gulf War*; Lanham, Maryland: University Press of America, 1991, pages 141-146. For more on the just war theory, see the reading list above.

3. See Franz Lieber, *A Code for the Government of Armies in the Field* (1863) and other military manuals, such as the U.S. Army field manual, *The Law of Land Warfare,* FM27-10 (1956).

4. VI *Hackworth's Digest of International Law* 266.

5. Max Hastings, *Bomber Command*; New York: Dial Press, 1979, page 170.

6. See a soldier's highly critical account: Alexander McKee, *Dresden 1945: The Devil's Tinderbox*; New York: E.P. Dutton, 1982.

7. Arthur Harris, *Bomber Offensive*; New York: Macmillan, 1947.

8. Wesley Craven and James Cate, *The Army Air Forces in World War II;* Chicago: University of Chicago Press, 1948-58, vol. 5, page 568.

9. Thomas M. Coffey, *Iron Eagle: The Turbulent Life of General Curtis LeMay*; New York: Crown Publishers, 1986, pages 133-134.

Week Three — What Has Been The Judgment Of History?

The berserker ethic avoids all criticism by one's comrades, who are only interested in enforcing the berserker's rule: no slacking, no holding back. But when the smoke clears, the judgment of history can be harsh.

Openers

How long has it been since something like a distant fire siren, or unexpected lightning, has made you rush to the radio to check the civil defense warning system?

At any time since 1945, have you ever said, or secretly thought, that using another atomic bomb might be a good idea?

Narrative And Comment

3. The judgment of history.

3.1. How did Americans react to Hiroshima and Nagasaki at the time?

The Gallup poll reported 85 percent approval of dropping the bomb. This was after the fact. Remember that the existence of the bomb was top secret before August 6, 1945.

But the approval was not unanimous. Hanson Baldwin, the strategic commentator for the *New York Times,* said:

> *Americans have become a synonym for destruction . . . .*
> *We have sowed the whirlwind . . . . We may yet reap the whirlwind . . . .*

New York Times, August 7, 1945.

The *New York Times* of August 10, 1945, reported a statement by the Federal Council of Churches asking that the atomic bombing stop to give the Japanese time to react. The statement was signed by Methodist Bishop G. Bromley Oxnam and the chairman of the Committee for a Just and Durable Peace, John Foster Dulles:

> *If we, a professedly Christian nation, feel morally free to use atomic energy in that way, men elsewhere will accept that verdict. Atomic weapons will be looked upon as a normal part of the arsenal of war and the stage will be set for the sudden and final destruction of mankind.*
>
> Quoted in Mark G. Toulouse, *The Transformation of John Foster Dulles*; Mercer, Georgia: Mercer University Press, 1985, page 110.

For eloquent contemporary condemnation of the bomb, go to *Commonweal* and *Christian Century* for August 1945. They reported, for instance, a sermon delivered the day after the second bomb by Rev. Bernard Iddings Bell at Trinity Episcopal Church, at the head of Wall Street:

> *To annihilate indiscriminately by the atomic bomb 100,000 persons at one shot, most of them civilians, women, little children, and then despite universal horror at us to repeat the performance yesterday at Nagasaki may be a military advisability, but victory so gained is bought at the price of world-wide moral revulsion against us . . . . [T]he silence of our Christian leaders in the past few days of moral crisis is in itself a measure of the decadence of American Christianity and of the magnitude of the task of her conversion.*
>
> *Christian Century,* August 29, 1945, page 982.

The prophetic minority spoke out loud and clear, but they were very few.

3.2. What became the "official" explanation of the use of the bomb?

Secretary of War Henry L. Stimson, by then retired and an elder statesman, published "The Decision to Use the

Atomic Bomb" in the February 1947 *Harper's Magazine*. He argued that the Japanese had been unstoppable fanatics, and their attempts to negotiate had been a sham. Stimson wrote: "... the major fighting would not end until the latter part of 1946, at the earliest. I was informed that such operations might be expected to cost over a million casualties, to American forces alone."

By the time Winston Churchill published his memoirs in 1953 these one million casualties had slid into one million deaths.[1] (The usual ratio is something like five casualties to each death.) Truman used a variety of numbers. His memoirs published in 1955 settled on "half a million American lives" as the number saved.[2]

These officials dismissed without discussion or ignored altogether all the roads-not-taken, such as warnings and threats, publicizing of the Alamogordo results, etc. They especially ignored the option of telling the Japanese they could keep the emperor, because that had eventually been done, but too late to prevent the two atomic bombings. The emperor had proven himself essential to stopping the fighting. No one was eager to try to explain why this road could not be taken in June or July of 1945, but only in August, after the bombs.

3.3. How has the "official" explanation stood up under critical scrutiny?

The historical works cited throughout this outline leave little to the "official" explanations but biographical claims of what the decision-makers may have been thinking at the time.

Even that has been questioned by some, notably by Gar Alperovitz in a book published in 1964.[3] Alperovitz believes that intimidation of the Soviet United was the sole reason for the bomb's use. Few scholars accept his theory fully, and it has caused much debate.

The general consensus has developed that the high officials overlooked many possibilities for a less violent end to the war and drove themselves into two acts of massive destruction that are hard to justify objectively. On the reasons for this there is less agreement. Students have found at least four ways of describing the Hiroshima and Nagasaki decisions: "A rational actor model, an organizational process model, a bureaucratic politics model and a war culture model."[4] Much depends on your perspective.

3.4. What has our political culture done with all this?

American political culture has ignored both the debate and the uncontroversial facts on which it rests. In our popular discourse the Japanese cities were bombed in an undelayable, forced, and unambiguous choice: Inflict 200,000 civilian deaths or accept 500,000 or more American military deaths. All other alternatives are ignored.

A culture that can obscure an issue like this can obscure anything. We have here a systematic bias where the reasons for violence are believed quickly and remembered long, even after they have been discredited, while the reasons for restraint are put to impossible standards of proof.

Scripture

And Dinah the daughter of Leah, which she bare unto Jacob, went out to see the daughters of the land. And when Shechem the son of Hamor the Hivite, prince of the country, saw her, he took her, and lay with her, and defiled her. And his soul clave unto Dinah the daughter of Jacob ...

(Jacob's sons offer an alliance: Shechem may have Dinah if all the men of his tribe will be circumcised.)

And unto Hamor and unto Shechem his son hearkened all that went out of the gate of his city; and every male was circumcised, all that went out of the gate of his city.

And it came to pass on the third day, when they were sore, that two of the sons of Jacob, Simeon and Levi,

Dinah's brethren, took each man his sword, and came upon the city boldly, and slew all the males. And they slew Hamor and Shechem his son with the edge of the sword, and took Dinah out of Shechem's house, and went out. The sons of Jacob came upon the slain, and spoiled the city, because they had defiled their sister. They took their sheep, and their oxen, and their asses, and that which was in the city, and that which was in the field. And all their wealth, and all their little ones, and their wives took they captive, and spoiled even all that was in the house.

And Jacob said to Simeon and Levi, "Ye have troubled me to make me to stink among the inhabitants of the land ..."

And they said, "Should he deal with our sister as with an harlot?"

— Genesis 34, KJV

David said to Solomon, "My son, I had planned to build a house to the name of the Lord my God. But the word of the Lord came to me, saying, 'You have shed much blood and have waged great wars; you shall not build a house to my name, because you have shed so much blood in my sight on the earth. See, a son shall be born to you; he shall be a man of peace. I will give him peace from all his enemies on every side; for his name shall be Solomon, and I will give peace and quiet to Israel in his days. He shall build a house for my name ....' "

— 1 Chronicles 22:7-10

Discussion Questions

Some people tend to find fault with public figures; some tend to defend public figures. What is your personal inclination? Do its origins lie in your life experiences, deep in your childhood, or what? Do you try to compensate for your personal inclination, or do you follow where it leads?

It is often said that those who fail to learn from the mistakes of history are condemned to repeat them. Is that true and relevant to this subject?

Do you perceive any overall direction to history? Is the world getting better, getting worse, or muddling along about the same? (Note: This question gets a lot easier if you limit it to specific subjects over specific time spans.)

References For Further Reading

The judgment of history is usually found in the same sources as those cited for facts and events, under Week One, above. Few historians care to give facts and events without a little judgment. For further thoughts:

Alperovitz, Gar. *Atomic Diplomacy: Hiroshima and Potsdam,* revised 1985 edition, with an introduction by the author answering his critics. Paperback $8.95. Viking Penguin, P.O. Box 120, Bergenfield, New Jersey 07621-0120. 1-800-526-0175. Alperovitz has more on this subject scheduled for publication in 1995.

Juhnke, William E., "Teaching the Atomic Bomb: The Greatest Thing in History," in *Nonviolent America: History Through the Eyes of Peace,* eds. Louise Hawkley and James C. Juhnke; North Newton, Kansas: Bethel College, 1993.

Footnotes

1. Winston Churchill, *Triumph and Tragedy;* Boston: Houghton Mifflin, 1953, page 638.

3. Harry S. Truman, *Memoirs*, vol. 1, *Year of Decisions;* Garden City, New York: Doubleday, 1955, page 417.

3. See *Atomic Diplomacy,* cited in the references, above.

4. James West Davidson and Mark Hamilton Lytle, "The Decision to Drop the Bomb: The Uses of Models in History," in *After the Fact: The Art of Historical Detection;* New York: McGraw Hill, 1992, discussed in William E. Juhnke, "Teaching the Atomic Bomb," above, pages 113-114.

Week Four — What Should Be The Judgment Of The Church?

How much, if at all, should the church concern itself with the affairs of the world? Much has been said and written on all sides of the question. It has been especially argued within the historic peace churches.

Openers

What was your denomination's attitude on slavery?

When has your local church or your denomination been too political, in your opinion? When has it not been involved enough?

What would happen to your Representative or your Senators if they came out for an immediate unilateral nuclear standdown?

Narrative And Comment

4. The judgment of the church.

4.1. Should the church have a judgment? Jesus said, "My kingdom is not of this world" (John 18:36 KJV).

There are both pacifisms of engagement and pacifisms of withdrawal.[1] There is "sectarian" pacifism, which "seeks to solve the problem of war and violence not for the world as a whole, but only for particular communities living lives withdrawn from some or all participation in the world," and there is "utopian" pacifism which "looks to the transformation of the world itself."[2] There is no reason to think that withdrawal from fighting in the conflicts of the world implies any reluctance to pass judgment on those conflicts.

For churches and individuals committed to the just war tradition, there would seem to be no avoiding the affairs of the world.

History does not suggest that the United States is in any danger of listening too closely to the church. Those few religiously sponsored reforms that succeeded — abolition of slavery, the civil rights movement, etc. — did so only by gaining a secular consensus. The historical record, while not entirely free of embarrassments, is generally one to encourage the church to speak out loud and clear on matters it deems lastingly important.

The more important reason for reluctance to judge is Jesus' admonition, "Judge not, that ye be not judged" (Matthew 7:1 KJV). We must take care to judge only things, not people — only acts, not actors. Some may believe it impossible to condemn a decision and not the decider. But if they refrain from judgment on that account, others will use their silence as endorsement of the decision itself. That has happened often enough with Hiroshima and Nagasaki, where a sensitive regard for the pressures and confusions of the time is often urged as a reason to approve of what was done under that pressure and confusion. (This seems to invert the logic of the situation, since it is under pressure and confusion that we would expect people to make the worst mistakes.)

The task of hating the sin and loving the sinner should not be beyond anyone well-versed in the facts of the atomic bombings. Americans at large did think the situation was a desperate one, much more desperate than it actually was.

4.2. Is there any hope that a sinful world will ever listen to the arguments of conscience?

One of the bellicist or pro-war distortions of our culture lies in forgetting, or never reporting in the first place, the numerous opportunities for war that America and other nations walk away from. E.g.: How many remember the pressures on Roosevelt to do something about Mexico in the 1930s, when the Mexican revolutionary government was confiscating petroleum reserves, which belonged to American and British oil companies, and lands belonging to the Catholic Church? Roosevelt compromised. That and other wars avoided are as important to our history as the wars accomplished. But the wars that explode get featured in the *Time-Life* history series, while we hear nothing of the wars avoided.

The point is not that governments can be trusted to do the right thing. The point is that they cannot always be trusted to do the wrong thing. This fact carries heavy moral implications. It leaves no room to evade the duty to witness for moderation, for restraint, for an even keel, even in the darkest hours.

4.3. If Christians give thought to such issues of bloodshed and physical conflict, do they not necessarily corrupt themselves, or at least waste their time?

What has been the experience of your own group? For three or four weeks you have been debating the killing of hundreds of thousands of people. Has this been good for your spiritual growth and maturity?

4.4. Does anyone who has not suffered the burdens of war have any right to sit in judgment on those who have?

The dramatic dialogue quotes some of Professor Paul Fussell's comments in the *New Republic*.[3] In that article Fussell also took a position common in discussions of peace and war: If you have not walked in a soldier's boots and carried a soldier's pack, and above all tasted a soldier's fear, your judgment on war may smack of righteousness. The observation has some truth — there is always the danger of pride in being right about anything. But experience shows it is not true that soldiering tends to make a bellicist.[4]

4.5. At least some Christians are called to live in the world. Are they not sometimes obliged to do hard things for a larger good?

It is morally wrong to stick needles into children and make them cry. Yet virtuous people do this regularly to inoculate children against diseases.

During World War II and the cold war many theologians, notably Reinhold Niebuhr, made a cult of this kind of necessity and began to write of "Christian irony" or "Christian realism," the need sometimes to do evil in order to do good.[5]

That is a central question here: Can "Christian realism," the complications and indirections of a virtuous life in a sinful world, ever include mass killings and maimings? Those tempted to say yes need to be warned: Some of the theologians who have gone down that path have not stopped short of the extermination of the human race. Paul Ramsey declares, "[We] have glimpsed the end of all things and seen there no 'specter' but the face of Jesus Christ," and therefore, Ramsey concludes, Christians cannot share the dread others feel at "the specter of the end of all things."[6] So Christian realism can be as dangerous as any other type of Christianity or realism.

4.6. Assume we have duly heeded the above objections and have decided to consider the rightness or wrongness of the use of the bomb. Is any citizen free to condemn any act so cherished by society? Could one go on living in a society after such a disagreement?

Much of the *Commentary* article mentioned in the dramatic dialogue was a polemic against guilt:

> *Even as the formal days of atonement in the Jewish and Christian calendar weaken, lose some of their traditional power, and attract fewer of the young to their rites, the age-old human impulse to critical self-scrutiny, with resulting acts of contrition to amend for past sins, takes on a new and secularized form. The date is August 6. Its icon is a mushroom cloud. The sin to be expiated is America's. And the event is Hiroshima ....*
>
> Andre Ryerson, "The Cult of Hiroshima," *Commentary* 80, October 1985, pages 36-40.

Most will agree that the idea of national guilt is wrong. The criminal law tends to be rather generous in dealing out collective guilt. Anyone who adheres to a conspiracy is responsible for everything done in the course of that conspiracy, whether the individual in question intended the thing or not. (The driver of a get-away car, for instance, can be convicted of murder for a killing during a robbery even if he or she expressly told the others not to hurt anyone.) But this is a pragmatic rule and often goes beyond our notions of moral guilt. Few of us feel much personal responsibility for acts done before we were born, or done in complete secrecy, or done over our vocal opposition.

It may be a form of bellicist bias to assume that society, ill-informed as it is, genuinely endorses the Hiroshima and Nagasaki bombings. The United States has signed the Nuclear Non-Proliferation Treaty, which obliges the nuclear powers "to pursue negotiations in good faith on effective measures relating to cessation of the nuclear arms race at an early date and to nuclear disarmament ...."[7]

There is this much basis for Fussell's charge of righteousness and Ryerson's charge of self-flagellation: The vast majority of nations on this earth own no nuclear weapons, do not want them, and have agreed not to construct any. At this writing, the governments of the United States and some of the former Soviet republics still own enough deliverable bombs for a world of Hiroshimas. For this suicidal peculiarity someone must bear some guilt. The bombs did not make themselves. And those who speak out against this state of affairs may well be tempted to feel somewhat righteous.

Scripture

> *I appeal to you therefore, brothers and sisters, by the mercies of God, to present your bodies as a living sacrifice, holy and acceptable to God, which is your spiritual worship. Do not be conformed to this world, but be transformed by the renewing of your minds, so that you may discern what is the will of God — what is good and acceptable and perfect.*
> — Romans 12:1-2

> *Let every person be subject to the governing authorities; for there is no authority except from God, and those authorities that exist have been instituted by God. Therefore whoever resists authority resists what God has appointed, and those who resist will incur judgment. For rulers are not a terror to good conduct, but to bad.*
> — Romans 13:1-3

> *But he perceived their craftiness and said to them, "Show me a denarius. Whose head and whose title does it bear?" They said, "The emperor's." He said to them, "Then give to the emperor the things that are the emperor's, and to God the things that are God's."*
> — Luke 20:23-25

Discussion Questions

Does your denomination have an official position on nuclear arms?

What do you judge to be the odds that your own life will be ended by an atomic weapon? Has your estimate of those odds changed much over the years?

References For Further Reading

On this question of the church in society, see:

Friesen, Duane K. *Christian Peacemaking and International Conflict: A Realist Pacifist Perspective;* 616 Walnut Avenue, Scottdale, Pennsylvania 15683: Herald Press, 1986.

_____. "Peacemaking as an Ethical Category," in *Ethics in the Nuclear Age,* ed. Todd Whitmore. Dallas: Southern Methodist University Press, 1989.

Ramsey, Paul, and Stanley Hauerwas. *Speak Up for Just War or Pacifism: A Critique of the United Methodist Bishops' Pastoral Letter "In Defense of Creation."* University Park, Pennsylvania: Pennsylvania State University Press, 1988.

Sharp, Gene. *The Politics of Non-violent Action.* Boston: Porter Sargent.

Stelmachowiicz, M. J., ed. *Peace and the Just War Tradition: Lutheran Perspectives in the Nuclear Age.* St. Louis: Concordia Press, 1987.

Footnotes

1. John Howard Yoder in his short but comprehensive book, *Nevertheless: A Meditation on the Varieties and Shortcomings of Religious Pacifism;* Scottdale, Pennsylvania: Herald Press, 1971, describes about 20 different schools of pacifism.

2. Roland Bainton, *Christian Attitudes Toward War and Peace;* Nashville: Abingdon Press, 1960, page xiii.

3. Paul Fussell, "Hiroshima: A Soldier's View," *The New Republic,* August 22 and 29, 1981.

4. See Fussell's own masterpieces about the two World Wars: *The Great War and Modern Memory;* New York: Oxford University Press, 1975, which is mostly about the literature and poetry that came out of World War I; and *Wartime: Understanding and Behavior in the Second World War;* New York: Oxford University Press, 1989, which deals with popular culture and thought in World War II. Or see any other account of how real soldiers have responded to real war.

5. See, e.g., Reinhold Niebuhr, *Beyond Tragedy: Essays in the Christian Interpretation of History;* New York: Scribner's, 1937 and *Christian Realism and Political Problems;* New York: Scribner's, 1953.

6. Paul Ramsey, *Speak up for Just War on Pacifism,* page 29.

7. Nuclear Non-Proliferation Treaty, Article VI.

Acknowledgements

Permission to use the following material has been granted and is gratefully acknowledged:

Page 13, Teller's speech. Quoted with permission from Edward Teller and Allen Brown, *The Legacy of Hiroshima;* Garden City, New York: Doubleday, 1962, pages 13-14.

Page 14, Bard: "I do not think the question ...." Used by permission of *U.S. News & World Report,* 2400 N. Street NW, Washington, D.C. 20037-1196.

Pages 17, 26-27, "Refusal to Mourn the Death, by Fire, of a Child in London." *Dylan Thomas: Collected Poems of Dylan Thomas,* copyright The Trustees of the Copyrights of Dylan Thomas. Used by permission of New Directions Publishing Corp.

Pages 17, haiku and tanka, quoted with permission from *The Atomic Bomb: Voices from Hiroshima and Nagasaki,* edited by Kyoko and Mark Selden; Armonk, New York: M.E. Sharpe, 1989, pages 137, 147-148.

Page 18, the Veteran. From Paul Fussell, "Hiroshima: A Soldier's View," *The New Republic,* August 22 and 29, 1981. Used by permission.

Page 19, the Commentator, and page 70. From Andre Ryerson, "The Cult of Hiroshima," *Commentary,* October 1985, pages 36-40. Used by permission, all rights reserved.

Pages 48-49, "I had specialized in gunnery ...." From *I was There,* by William D. Leahy, pages 440-441. Copyright Ayer Press, P.O. Box 958, Salem, New Hampshire 03079, used by permission.

Page 62, quotation from the August 29, 1945 issue of *Christian Century.* Copyright 1945 Christian Century Foundation, 407 South Dearborn Street, Chicago, Illinois 60605-1105, used by permission.

Index

Alamogordo test	43, 63
Alperovitz, Gar	63
Atomic Energy Commission	21
Baldwin, Hanson	61
Balloon bombs	16, 26
Bard, Ralph A.,	
Undersecretary of	9, 13-14,
the Navy	24, 47, 50
Bell, Bernard Iddings	62
Bell, George Kennedy,	
Bishop of Chichester	7
Bhagavad-Gita	22
Bohr, Niels	12, 23
Bombing, conventional	7, 54-56, 59
Brewster, Oswald C.	9, 11, 12-13, 23
Buddha	16
Bush, George, President	54
Casualties and deaths	
from a possible	15, 18, 25,
invasion of Japan	46-47, 52n, 63
Christian Century	62
Christian irony or	
realism	69-70
Chronology of World	
War II, brief	42-43
Church, political	
judgments of	67-73
Churchill, Winston	63
Columbus, 500th	
anniversary	7
Commentary	9, 18-19, 28, 70
Commentator	
(Andre Ryerson)	9, 18-19, 28, 70
Commonweal	62
Costumes	11
Cranes, paper	16, 25
Doolittle, James,	
raid on Tokyo	55
Dresden, destruction of	55
Dulles, Allen	44
Dulles, John Foster	62

Einstein, Albert	7, 9, 12-20, 22-23, 25, 31
Eisenhower, Dwight D.	48
Emperor of Japan. *See*	
Japan, Emperor	
Federal Council of	
Churches	61
Fermi, Enrico	23
Forrestal, James	45
Franck, James O.,	13, 23-24,
and Franck Report	47-48, 50
Frisch, Otto	12
Fussell, Paul	27, 69, 73
Gallup poll	61
Groves, Leslie R.,	
quoted on Szilard	24
Guilt, collective	
or national	7, 19, 70
Hansell, Haywood, Jr.	56
Harris, Sir Arthur,	
chief of RAF Bomber	
Command	55
Hiroshima and Nagasaki,	
people of	9, 15-20, 27
Hitler, Adolf	7-8
Holocaust	7-8
Honshu, planned	
invasion of. *See*	
Casualties and deaths	
House of Lords, Bishop	
Bell's speech in	7
Hydrogen bomb	21, 24
Hymns suggested	30, 34, 36, 38, 39
Interim Committee on	
Atomic Energy	14
International control	
of atomic energy	24
Invasion of Japan	
See Casualties and	
deaths	

Japan
   Blockade of   14
   Coded messages
      intercepted   45
   Emperor   14, 43-46, 63
   Invasion of. *See*
      Casualties and deaths
   Militarism   43
   Peace party   32, 43-46
Jeptha's daughter,
   sacrificing of   33-34
Jesus of Nazareth,
   the "Host"   9, 11, 15-20
Just war tradition   53-54, 58

Kaiser Wilhelm Institute,
   Berlin   12, 23
Kamikazes   43
Kyushu, planned
   invasion of. *See*
   Casualties and deaths

Leahy, William D.   48-49
LeMay, Curtis   56
"London's Daughter,"
   child killed in the
   Blitz   9, 16-20, 26-27

Marshall, George C.   15
McCloy, John J.   45
Meitner, Lise   9, 12, 23

Nagasaki, people of. *See*
   Hiroshima and Nagasaki,
   people of
Nagasaki bomb,
   timing of   49
Nazis, possibility of
   getting atomic bomb   12, 21, 22
New Republic   18, 69
Niebuhr, Reinhold   69-70
Nuclear fission,
   discovery of   23, 42
Nuclear Non-Proliferation
   Treaty   71

Okinawa casualties   47

Oppenheimer, J. Robert,
   scientific director of   7, 9, 12-20,
   the Manhattan Project   21-22, 31
Oxnam, G. Bromley,
   Methodist Bishop   62

Pacifism   53, 57-58, 67
Peace faction within the
   Japanese government.
   See Japan, Peace party
Peace feelers from Japan.
   See Japan, Peace party
Pearl Harbor   42
Peierls, Rudolf   9, 14, 24-25
Pride, danger of   70-71
Props listed   10

Rabi, Isador I.   21
Ramsey, Paul   70
Roosevelt, Franklin D.
   Einstein's letter to   12, 22-23, 31
   Friction with Mexico   68
Russia (USSR)   14, 63
Ryerson, Andre   28, 70

Sasaki, Sadako   9, 11, 15-20, 25
Scenery   11
Seinosuke, Taniguchi,
   haiku by   17, 27
Soviet Union.
   See Russia
Stimson, Henry L.   13, 62-63
Stone, I.F.   46
Surrender of Japan
   Possibility at time the
   bomb was used.
   See Japan, Peace party
Szilard, Leo   13, 24

Teller, Edward   9, 11, 13, 21, 24
Thirty Seconds Over
   Tokyo   55
Thomas, Dylan   16-20, 26-27
Threat or warning of
   bomb's use
      Urged by Bard   13-14
      Urged by Franck   23-24

Toshikazu, Masuoka,
  tanka by   17, 27
Toshiyuki, Numata,
  haiku by   17, 27
Truman, Harry S.,
  President   13, 15, 25, 42, 63
U.S.S.R. *See Russia*
United States Strategic
  Bombing Survey   44
Veteran   9, 18, 27
Warning of bomb's use.
  See Threat or warning

Scripture References

Old Testament

Genesis 34	64
Deuteronomy 5:17	56
Judges 11:30-32, 34-39	32-33
2 Samuel 12:23	31
1 Chronicles 22:7-10	65
Psalm 40:11	29
Psalm 120	33-34
Psalm 130	33
Isaiah 11:6-10	56-59
Jonah 4:9-11	49

New Testament

Matthew 7:1	68
Matthew 22:34-40	35
Matthew 25:34-40	35
Matthew 26:51-52	57
Mark 14:47	57
Luke 20:23-25	72
Luke 22:49-51	57
John 11:35	49
John 18:10-11	57
John 18:36	67
Romans 12:1-2	71
Romans 13:1-3	72
Revelation 14:17-20	34